Healthy Eating

by Helen Gregory

Consultant:
Adria F. Klein, PhD
California State University, San Bernardino

CAPSTONE PRESS
a capstone imprint

Wonder Readers are published by Capstone Press,
1710 Roe Crest Drive, North Mankato, Minnesota 56003.
www.capstonepub.com

Library of Congress Cataloging-in-Publication Data
Gregory, Helen.
  Healthy eating / Helen Gregory.—1st ed.
    p. cm.—(Wonder readers)
  Includes index.
  ISBN 978-1-4765-0036-2 (library binding)
  ISBN 978-1-4296-7828-5 (paperback)
  ISBN 978-1-4765-0849-8 (eBook pdf)
  1. Nutrition—Juvenile literature. I. Title. II. Series.
  RA784.G759 2013
  613.2—dc23   2011023094

Summary: Introduces readers to the four food groups and explains why eating healthy is important.

Editorial Credits
Maryellen Gregoire, project director; Mary Lindeen, consulting editor; Gene Bentdahl, designer;
Sarah Schuette, editor; Wanda Winch, media researcher; Eric Manske, production specialist

Photo Credits
Capstone Studio: Karon Dubke

Word Count: **211**   Guided Reading Level: **I**   Early Intervention Level: **16**

Printed in China.
092012   006934LEOS13

Table of Contents

Note to Parents and Teachers

The Wonder Readers Next Steps: Science series supports national science standards. These titles use text structures that support early readers, specifically with a close photo/text match and glossary. Each book is perfectly leveled to support the reader at the right reading level, and the topics are of high interest. Early readers will gain success when they are presented with a book that is of interest to them and is written at the appropriate level.

Food

Food gives your body **energy**
for playing soccer or jumping
in a sack race.

Your body needs different kinds of food to be healthy.

Grains

Food is divided into five groups.
One of these is the grain group.

Eating whole grains such as whole wheat pasta, oatmeal, and popcorn is healthy for you. Start your day with a bowl of whole-grain cereal!

Fruits and Vegetables

Another group is the fruit group.
Fruits are full of **vitamins**.

Vitamins help you grow,
keep your teeth healthy,
and heal sores.

Another group is
the vegetable group.
Vegetables have vitamins too.
They also have **fiber**.

Fiber helps your body run better.
The most colorful vegetables
are the most healthy for you.

Proteins

Meat, **poultry**, fish, beans, and eggs make up the **protein** group.

Proteins build strong bones, skin, and muscles. Nuts are a good source of protein.

Dairy Foods

Dairy foods are the last group.
Milk, yogurt, and cheese
are all dairy foods.

Dairy foods keep your teeth
and bones strong.
Choose low-fat milk, cheese,
or yogurt.

Other Foods

Oils are not a food group,
but you need some every day.
You can get healthy oils
from fish and nuts.

Sometimes you can sneak in a treat.
Try picking healthy snacks too!

You should eat food from all
of the food groups every day.

Now Try This!

Time to make a pie graph! First draw a circle. Now think back to the last meal you had. How much of your meal came from the protein group and the dairy group? How much came from the fruit and vegetable groups and the grain group? Did any of your foods count as "other?" Divide your circle up into sections that represent how much of your food came from each food group.

Glossary

energy   the strength to do active things without getting tired

fiber   a part of food that passes through the body but is not digested

poultry   birds such as chickens, turkeys, or geese

protein   a substance found in foods such as meat, cheese, eggs, and fish

vitamin   a nutrient that helps keep people healthy

Internet Sites

FactHound offers a safe, fun way to find Internet sites related to this book. All of the sites on FactHound have been researched by our staff.

Here's all you do:

Visit *www.facthound.com*

Type in this code: 9781476500362

Check out projects, games and lots more at
www.capstonekids.com

Index